The Art of
Outdoor Living

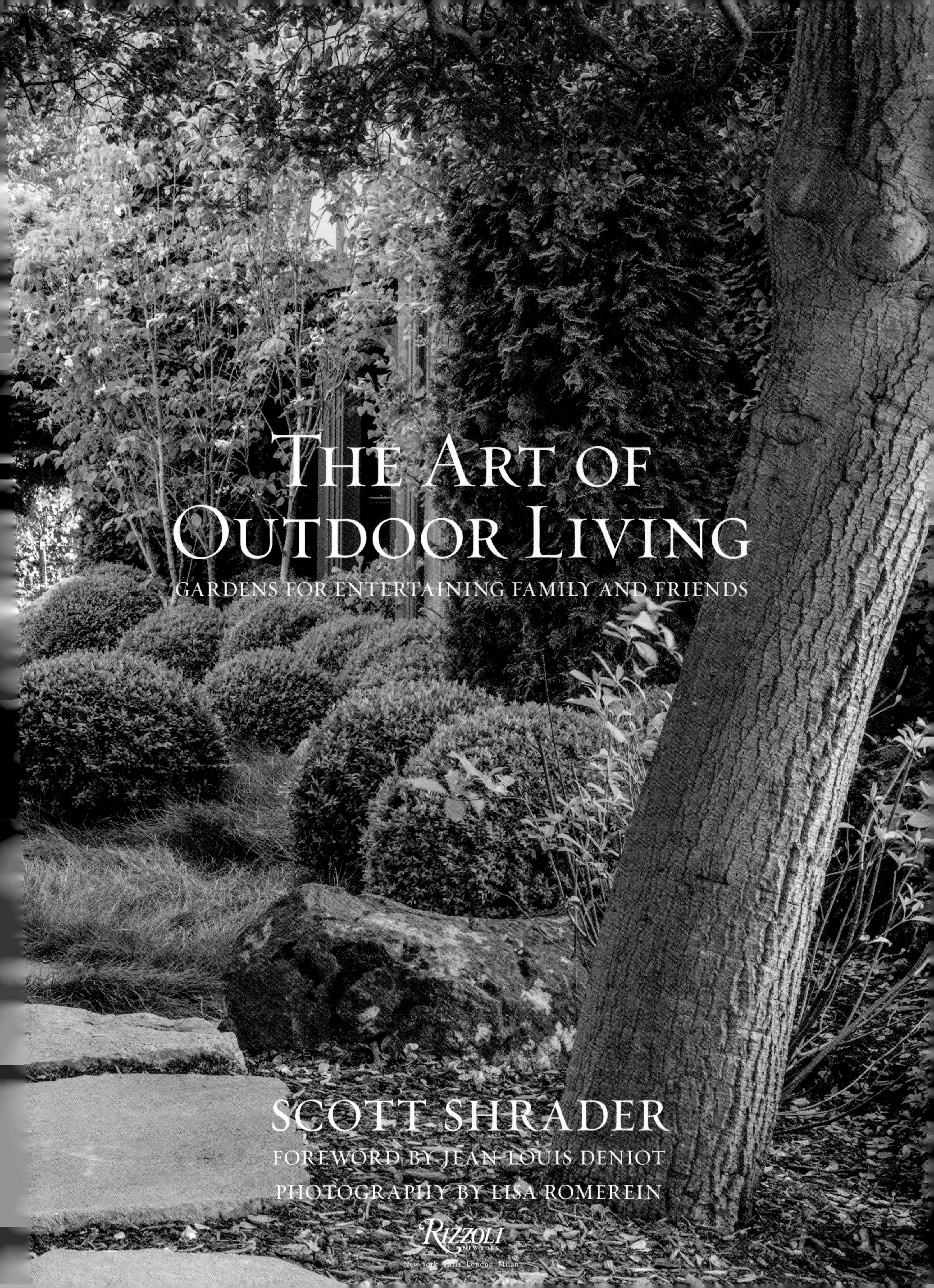

The Art of Outdoor Living

GARDENS FOR ENTERTAINING FAMILY AND FRIENDS

SCOTT SHRADER

FOREWORD BY JEAN-LOUIS DENIOT

PHOTOGRAPHY BY LISA ROMEREIN

RIZZOLI
NEW YORK

New York Paris London Milan

To Roxy, my beloved dog, truly man's best friend

TABLE OF CONTENTS

FOREWORD

The first images that come to mind when people think of Los Angeles may be strip malls and traffic, but they are the last things I associate with the city.

I am lucky enough to have a Scott Shrader garden in Los Angeles. And I should specify that this is a garden Scott literally created from nothing. I knew it was not Scott's dream project, but after I saw images of his work and then had the pleasure of getting further acquainted with him, I knew that his aesthetic and mine would blend, and that he was the one to be entrusted with this task. I convinced him to take it on.

Scott took very difficult, overgrown, steep terrain and reinvented it, turning the entire hillside into a living tribute to everything there is to love about the Los Angeles climate and lifestyle.

He created seven different seating areas amid the landscape, playing with the perspectives provided by the hillside, and turned every square foot into a multisensory experience, all in keeping with his unique design integrity.

There truly is something special about the famous Los Angeles sunlight. Its sharpness creates beautiful shapes, almost like shadow puppetry, and when it hits the watered ground and plants, the most intoxicating scents of fresh greenery and wet sand are emitted.

A garden reunites all elements of nature—from the plants, leaves, flowers, and their fragrance to the insects and birds that visit. There are the sounds of the wind passing through leaves and the soft crunch of round gravel pebbles underfoot, the crackling of an outdoor fire, the songs of water features, discreetly hidden to provide a backdrop just loud enough to muffle the noise of cars and neighbors.

What I love about Scott's work is that nothing is ever overdone. His work is very graphic and may look simple at first glance, but there is a high level of sophistication. Nothing is coincidental, but nothing is forced. His carefully understated hand allows all elements of nature to complement each other, giving the illusion that everything grew together naturally.

The base of his work is so strong that the colors and textures of the vegetation and the leaves themselves are more than enough to create depth and magic. His ability to integrate lighting and sound systems so seamlessly makes for a final result that provides a truly transporting experience, and a complement to the interiors in every way.

As an interior designer and architect, I identify with the approach Scott brings to his projects and find intrinsic similarities between my work and landscape design.

You start with a layout, then move from there to imagine the space in elevations, developing the various perspectives. Where I would complete my vision with interior details and furnishing, in landscaping it is a question of specifying the plant species that will achieve the intended composition, scale, contemplation, and overall volumes.

Style-wise, the landscaping vocabulary has as much variety as that of architecture and interior design: manicured European style, English, Spanish, tropical, minimal, desertscapes . . . . The overall landscape style and its specific flora must correspond to the location and architecture of a property, just as the interiors must be cohesive with a property's locale and exterior aesthetic.

In some ways, creating a garden is like building an entire second house; the outdoor lifestyle, when masterfully done, should function on its own and make you forget about the interiors. You know this has been achieved when you almost prefer the outdoors to the indoors!

As an interior designer, my work is always inspired by a home's immediate surroundings, its environment and views—my design intentions are an extension of those elements.

There is one major difference, however: time. While time has little effect on interior design and decor aside from fostering the development of patina, it wields considerable impact on a garden's actual physical shape. It takes great talent, foresight, and planning to imagine how a garden will evolve over the next ten, twenty, fifty years!

Nothing can compare to nature's beauty and its power to inspire contemplation and enjoyment. Scott is gifted at bringing out the best in nature and adding his director's touch while fully respecting the environment. He does this through his superb understanding of flora and fauna, his love, his hard work, his keen eye for the very fine-tuned balance between all the elements he adds. Looking at it another way, Scott builds each of his masterpieces the way a writer composes a script: he sets a solid framework, then spikes the scenarios with cinematic points of view.

I see Scott as a minimal maximalist. His work is the epitome of "just enough." It gives the exact right amount of everything, while still feeling highly generous. Scott's talent is such that he does not need to distract the observer with bright flowers and colors to make his gardens captivating, transcendent, extraordinary!

The work we do as designers is highly personal. The greatest gift we can give our clients is a sense of happiness and enrichment through the environments we create, and Scott has given that to many lucky people, including myself. Scott's work is beyond a talent or a service. Indeed, it is beyond special. He creates osmosis, magic, and poetry by invoking life through exquisitely composed nature.

—Jean-Louis Deniot

INTRODUCTION

Landscapes and gardens are different from interiors. They mature. They change constantly in small ways, shifting mood with the light and the weather, transforming dramatically with the cycling of the seasons and the passage of years. Rooms, on the other hand, remain fairly consistent. Yes, the quality of sunlight and artificial illumination affects the atmosphere of our indoor spaces, but not nearly as much as that of a garden. When a house is done, typically it is done. We can alter the mood of an interior with accessories, art, flowers, and holiday decorations. For the most part, though, the sofa is the sofa. It will not go deciduous—or bloom.

Time means everything in our outdoor environments. Because we relax in them, they seem to take us out of time. Because they are alive, they are in a constant state of flux within the fixed boundaries of the hardscape we design. And we always have to plan for growth and evolution: how tall, broad, and wide the plant material needs to become to realize the vision, and how it will mature.

For as long as I can remember, I have had an interest in having my hands in the earth. I grew up on the Palos Verdes Peninsula, a suburb of Los Angeles, in a beautiful house that my mother created and cared for with energy and passion. My mother loves to garden and has always kept her well-designed, professionally landscaped yard perfectly tended. (I believe I get my eye for balance, scale, and placement from her.) My father, an orthopedic surgeon and adventure enthusiast, was very interested in organic gardening, as was my grandfather, and they indulged that interest at our weekend ranch house in Coto de Caza in Orange County, south of Los Angeles. From the time we were able, my brother and I were out in the yard with them, planting, building walls, installing irrigation systems, and so on.

When I was growing up, my father also had twenty acres of orange groves in Escondido that he had planted himself. On weekends, he, my grandfather, my brother, and I would drive the two hours down the coast to pick oranges all day and then drive back with a station wagon full of fruit to share with our neighbors in Palos Verdes. I can still remember the weight of the big, full, burlap bags hanging off my back. My father later came to be friends with a beekeeper. After he inherited all the equipment for tending the hives and taking care of the bees, we established more than twenty hives in the middle of the grove to pollinate the citrus. We would go down to rob the bees, bring all the equipment back to the ranch house to clean and repaint it, and then spin the honey, which we labeled Shrader Sting. Our neighbors in Palos Verdes gave us their old mayonnaise jars, which we returned filled with honey. (We even had a special version with honeycomb.) These experiences opened my eyes early to nature and her cycles.

I cannot really remember a time when I did not want to grow things myself, or when I wasn't drawing and creating other art projects. My parents let me start experimenting with gardens and planting early. And when I was ten or eleven, they bought me a small hydroponic garden so I could tend plants off our balcony. (They wanted to keep me out of their professionally landscaped garden.) This balcony garden was my own little paradise of carrots, radishes, and other quick-growing things meant to satisfy my childhood obsession—and it's a source of very fond memories. Every morning and again after school, I would watch, wait, and wonder when the little sprouts were going to pop up through the soil.

When we were at our ranch house in Coto de Caza, my parents would take me to Roger's Gardens in Corona del Mar, a legend in the nursery world. We would wander slowly through the nursery, which seemed to go on for acres. I would memorize the layout, plantings, and arrangements of plants in pots. Once we got back to Palos Verdes, I would recreate the areas and arrangements that had caught our eye. To this day, my visual memory works as it did then: I can walk through a place once and, back in the car, draw it exactly to one-quarter scale.

Thinking I would go into real estate development, I majored in urban planning at the University of Southern California. But after working for a bank for four years doing feasibility studies for development projects, I knew enough to be sure that a graduate degree in finance, the next step for that career, was not my future. My eureka moment came when a friend told me about a friend of his who had left his job to pursue a graduate degree in landscape design at Cal Poly Pomona.

The program at Cal Poly Pomona is incredibly selective, extremely rigorous, and, even then, focused on ecology and sustainability. In my day, the faculty included many interesting and notable instructors. John T. Lyle, an early guru of sustainable landscape design, was one such luminary. Robert Perry, the widely recognized authority on the use of landscape plants

and water conservation in semi-arid zones of California, was another. Our graduate studios centered on large-scale environments—watersheds, Yosemite National Park, historical studies of the Ice Age and water flow, and so on—because the school was training people to go into city agencies and carry on its ecology-based approach to design. I loved the program, and it taught me to take in large-scale projects and to be comfortable with plans on a vast scale. My real interest, however, was in residential design, so I was something of a fish out of water.

The first week out of graduate school, I met Lani Berrington, a Cal Poly Pomona alum with an A-list clientele, including Lionel Richie, Mel Gibson, and Cher, just to name a few. Lani happened to be landscaping the yard of the house across the street from my parents' house in Palos Verdes. Though I had several projects of my own already, she needed help. And I could draw.

Lani and I worked together for five years. She taught me the profession: how to take a project from beginning to end in practical and business terms. Just as importantly, she introduced me to an entirely new world of planting. Generally, a garden designer plans for plantings to mature over seven, eight, or even ten years. But when the budget permits a certain scale of plant materials—as Lani's budgets did—it is possible to create a garden within six months or a year that looks as if it has been coming into its own for a lifetime. Lani helped train my eye to work at that scale.

Through Lani, I also met Ruben Vazquez and his son Mariano, who installed the gardens we designed with great attention to detail. Lani and Ruben had been working together since the 1960s, and Mariano joined the team when he came of age. She and I agreed that they could help me install my side projects, provided her gardens always took precedence. When she later closed her office, they joined me. Now Ruben has retired. Mariano, who took over, has helped me complete hundreds of gardens over the last twenty-five years or more.

Every property comes with its unique set of challenges. For me, the house almost always dictates the style of the garden. My role, in part, is to hide the bad assets, like utility poles, and highlight the good assets. This involves a process of discovery. The first thing I do is listen to the house and what it wants and needs. I stand back, look, and assess what its great features are and what it is missing. This visual dialogue helps me to develop the story I will use to shape the design. As I tell my clients, "Everything you see and feel getting to the front door sets the tone and says a lot about who lives behind it."

In these early stages of getting to know the place and my clients, I also want to hear immediately what my clients think does and does not work about the interior and exterior environments, and about the relationship between the two. Would they consider moving the front door? Opening up a wall with French doors? Creating a parking area or courtyard to hide the car from the interior view? Most of my clients live in and around Los Angeles. They are in their cars all the time. When they are at home, do they really want to look out the window and see a car?

My role as a designer of exterior spaces—landscapes and gardens—is to extend the elements of style, character, and personal expression from the architecture and interiors of the house into the designed environments out of doors. The entire property, in my view, should look as though it is the result of a single creative vision, as if one hand and mind were responsible for every last detail. This is even more true with historic estates where elements of the original gardens survive. When I am finished with the grounds of this type of property, I want them to look as they once were, or might have been, or at the very least carry into the present the spirit of their past.

Gardens are for living in, not just for looking at from the other side of a window. I want the environments I create to be visually alluring, but also, and more importantly, to be so incredibly comfortable and functional that they draw my clients out of doors and keep them there, relaxing, reading, eating, entertaining, whether alone or with family and friends. I furnish these exteriors as I would an interior room, with appropriate seating and tables grouped for ease and placed so everyone has a great view at all times from every angle.

I usually start a project inside the home and move outward because I focus on the transitions between the indoor and outdoor environments. What is the best design and material solution for going from a very dark floor to a light one? How can I blend the two seamlessly in terms of color, texture, and feel? The experience of moving between the indoors and outdoors should feel like a great yoga class, one where the poses have been choreographed to flow organically from one to the next.

My gardens tend to be rich in greens, but limited otherwise in their palettes of color, texture, and shape. Often I use no additional color at all, and only three or four plant materials massed in clear groupings. If I do use colors other than green, I choose one or two and stick with those. Visual simplicity has great power. Consistency seems to calm the eye and soothe the spirit, while variety feels erratic.

By their very nature, gardens take us out of our everyday worlds. They are our private oases, the safe, beautiful places we create for ourselves to retreat, relax, and recharge. When they are designed, arranged, and lit for atmosphere and ambience so that we can use them to share a wonderful meal, a quiet afternoon, or a fabulous celebration with family and friends, there is nothing better. I would rather be inside a garden than inside my home, so creating environments that make memorable outdoor moments possible for others brings me great happiness. I feel privileged to be a designer of exteriors, a shaper of landscapes and gardens. And I come alive when I see properties changing, finding their beauty, and bringing people joy.

PART I
PRINCIPLES OF DESIGN

SUSTAINABILITY

Gardens are beautiful, emerging, living beings. They need care, maintenance, and love, just like we do. Also, just like us, they show up, stand at attention, and perform when they are happy in their surroundings, well fed, and well tended. Each is its own micro ecosystem with its personal set of climate and soil conditions. Even in Southern California, where the climate is exceptionally friendly, there are only so many species of plant materials that will thrive in a given place when water is a concern. A garden's ecology is everything. Is it on rock, sand, or clay? Does it require heavy soil excavation? Is there a lot of salt in the air? Is the temperature range constant or not? Is it watered from a well or some other source? Only when I understand the specific environment can I begin to design the exterior spaces and select an appropriate plant palette.

From an early age, I gardened with both my parents and my grandfather. My mother has a keen eye for beauty and an innate sense of scale and proportion. Both my grandfather and father have a natural instinct for working on and with the land. My grandfather, in particular, focused on growing things organically and sustainably, so we always mulched and composted. One year we might plant his entire garden with wheatgrass, let it go to seed, and then till it into the soil to enrich it. When we went to Mexico to fish, we would cut up the carcasses, bring them home, and use them as fertilizer. From the time I could spade and hoe, I was thinking about nature and her systems.

My later training at Cal Poly Pomona reinforced this focus on sustainability. Long before changes were made to our city codes to mandate water-efficient landscapes in Los Angeles after our last major drought, I encouraged my clients to use lawns less, to reclaim and retain as much water on site as possible (in some areas of Los Angeles it is now illegal to drain water off site), and to tend their gardens organically, without elaborate feeding, pesticide, or watering programs.

Time plays a role in the creation of a sustainable garden, and not just in the most obvious way. Knowing how long my clients plan to stay on their property helps me determine how to phase the project and what size plant materials are needed. Gardens also require constant attention and maintenance. Every plant grows on its own schedule. Some demand regular weekly or monthly trims, while others can look and grow their best if they come under the shears four times a year, or even once a year. These basic practicalities factor into how I conceive the spaces and plantings and plan the best way to care for them.

A professor once told me to think about plants as people—as my friends—and to select the living materials for a garden as if I were having a party and throwing a group together. Some like to drink. Some are teetotalers. Some like to bask in the sun. Some need to be in the shade. Some play well with others. Some prefer to be by themselves. Some bloom. Others do not. Still others go dormant. I love dissecting the properties of plants in that fundamental, personalized way. And I love selecting, placing, and caring for them so that they feel at home and perform at their best to complement a house and enhance a client's life.

THE OUTDOOR LIFESTYLE

From my point of view, to experience a garden means to live in it. This is why function and comfort matter in the exterior spaces just as much as they do within the house. Of course I want to direct the view to something beautiful. But most of all, once a garden has drawn people out of the house, I want to keep them there. So there has to be comfortable seating. And convenient places to put down a drink. And some element of warmth—a fireplace, fire pit, or heater—so that they do not rush right back inside.

I tend to emphasize the axial views—from the front door through the house, from the living room to the side views, and so on. This visual orientation is logical and comfortable in almost every situation. Usually, I create a central focal point at moments of entry. Often these use fire or water, because those are real attractors. We all gravitate toward water. We also all love to sit by a fire. And depending on the fire source, I can arrange the seating in a wide variety of ways.

In the outdoors, as inside, lighting helps to define space, atmosphere, and mood. For the outdoors to feel warm and inviting, not ominous and black, it needs to be well lit. Tall trees and trellises are wonderful places to hide a variety of light sources. I like the magical effect of the illumination, and also the different illusions that hidden lighting, especially when it is on dimmers, can create. Finding your way through a property where various light sources are illuminated is a happier and more interesting experience than simply following a series of path lights—which can make a path look like a landing strip at LAX.

Typically, people feel most comfortable when they have some form of covering overhead, such as an umbrella, a tree, or a trellis. These outdoor ceilings provide a sense of shelter and shade. They are crucial not only because they create a sense of human scale under the endless sky, but also because they provide a means for hiding lights and space heaters. A formation of trees with outstretched branches can also serve this purpose. So can the overhang of an eave. Umbrellas and trellises are common and beautiful options. I like to be able to see the sky, so I tend to leave my trellises somewhat open. I build them out of steel, and then I feed the lighting up through components so that the wires are invisible.

Pizza ovens are a main event, a celebration of friends and food. Everyone wants to gather around a pizza oven, just as people tend to congregate in the kitchen when the party's inside. I like to include areas for people to hang out and help, or just talk, right near the area where the prep work takes place. The sink needs to be convenient, as does the refrigerator. This is the spot that I call the "command post." I usually put it behind a stool-height counter, so guests can sit on stools and chat with the host. I also make sure that the sight lines to other areas of the garden are clear, so the host can keep an eye on the other activities nearby.

To plan exterior spaces, I first go through the interior of the house to understand how it functions and flows. Then I plan the different areas from the inside out. I may suggest ways to open up the rooms—removing a wall, putting in French doors—to create more gracious exits into the gardens and to establish focal points that enhance the interiors and also draw people out of doors.

To organize the backyard, I always walk the property to find the best angle or perspective on the house from the farthest away spot. Then I start placing the various functional spaces around that point, establishing my lounge area or built-in banquette seating there to draw people into the garden's far reaches. (If this lounge area is not going to be the yard's focal point I may tuck it off to the side.) Wherever there is seating, I make sure it faces a beautiful view.

If the garden is not comfortable and does not function smoothly, everyone turns around and goes right back into the house. Enjoying time with family, friends, and food in the garden is another level of experience. Why not make it the most we can imagine it to be?

NAVIGATING THE TERRAIN

My father put my brother and me on skis early, and we were heli-skiing by the time I was in my mid-teens. Over the years, we have traversed nearly two million vertical feet of mountain terrain together in British Columbia, including the infamous, steep, heavily forested region known as the Monashees, the glaciers of the Bugaboos, and the highlands, forest groves, canyons, and plateaus of the Cariboos. I feel sure this has affected my sense of space and the way I approach the design of landscapes. Certainly it has influenced my understanding of the effects of rise and fall, of vistas that narrow and open, of the surprise reveal of a meadow coming through a stand of trees. Good skiers follow the fall line. We have to be able to read a mountain to see and navigate a pathway down it. Our eyes must stay focused forward to perceive upcoming hazards like crevasses, wells, outcroppings, stands of trees, and cliffs. Over time, good skiers develop an almost sixth sense for terrain: how a mountain pitches left and right, where its knolls are, where to plant the poles to make a turn, how to cut a beautiful pathway through the randomness of a particular landscape.

All of this translates into the opening and closing of spaces on a property that can set a tone for an entry, an exit, or a contemplative moment. There is a sequence and a rhythm to an exterior pathway. I often put something at the end to act as a draw or a focal point. Just as important is the experience along the way created by the scale of the different plant materials. Whether I am designing a route in my mind as I stand on a property or drawing it on paper in my studio, I am able to see it in three dimensions and envision how it will look when it is planted and mature with hardscape (a catchall term for what's underfoot) features and/or gravel in place. I know that as I walk along it, at a certain point I need something tall on my left to block out a neighbor's house and something else on my right to draw the eye. To move people through the space, I give them little moments of difference and beauty to capture their interest and attention along the way.

Every design decision I make depends on the purpose of the passageway and the spaces and places it connects. Does it lead from the sidewalk to the front door? From the back door out to the pool? To the guesthouse? I start from the ground up, selecting, choosing, and placing my hardscape materials depending on the mood and feeling I want to establish. For more earthy, casual yet chic, and comfortable gardens, I tend to use gravel because it sounds, looks, and feels very comforting. It is also sustainable and very beautiful with more exotic items, such as reclaimed stone from Italy or repurposed brick from a Chinese wall. Even in a hardscape that incorporates intricate patterns, I prefer connecting pathways in gravel.

The more materials and textures a space includes, the more active it feels to me. I often whittle the palette of a garden down to five materials: three plants, one hardscape, and gravel. The combination is visual simplicity itself, bringing calm and heightened awareness to the setting.

The plant palette tends to be one of the last elements I consider. Planting a garden is very much like creating an interior, except with plants we have to plan for the future. Gardens are all about change, so it is key to understand how tall the trees we put in will eventually be and how to place things so that they grow well on their own and with the neighboring plants. My goal is to plant a garden once and then allow it to mature, becoming what it wants to become, with the hope that it will last for generations.

PART II
THE GARDENS

MY LABORATORY

People have asked why a landscape designer would want a house with such limited garden spaces. The explanation is simple: It is both my playground and my refuge, and I can maintain it myself in the time I have available. This house and garden are the perfect place for testing out new ideas and combinations. While I am tinkering, snipping, and moving plants around, the rest of the world disappears.

When I found the house where I now live almost two decades ago, it was basically a shell. It happened to be in a neighborhood I loved—the Norma Triangle, right in the heart of West Hollywood. Legend has it that Norma Talmadge, the silent screen siren, had her studios here. The bungalows had been forgotten for a while, then dolled up again later with false fronts during the Hollywood Regency era. The houses were very modestly sized, which was perfect for my needs. As a further plus, this one had eleven-foot ceilings and great potential for creating a direct connection to the outdoors. By simply removing a few walls and replacing all the doors and windows with ten-foot French doors, I was able to open up each room to its own special view and an attached functional outdoor environment. To underscore the transition to the chiseled stone that I was using to pave the yard, I stained the oak floors of the interior a rich, dark chocolate.

After banishing the cypresses that circled the property when I bought it, I put in dense ficus hedges to enclose it. The rear garden measures forty-five feet by twenty-five feet. Lifting this space up by three feet and filling it in so it was all on one level made the entire property feel more expansive. My husband, Mark Hemphill, and I wanted be able to cook outdoors and entertain friends. Because I needed the very limited area to serve many different functions, I divided it into three distinct environments—dining in the center; outdoor kitchen with pizza oven on the left; lounge and fire pit on the right. A reflective pond lined in sheet bronze backs up to the dining area, adding depth, dimension, and scale. I have filled it with shubunkin (a Japanese goldfish). It also hosts a sculpture of Icarus commissioned from Simon Toparovsky that appears to float, as well as aquatic plants that I change with the seasons. Two olive trees planted in this area early on have matured in the years I have lived here. They provide beautiful ambience for the dining area and handy armatures for hidden lighting. The pair of olive trees has also become a wonderful shading device; they protect the interior against the direct summer sun, which allows us to leave the French doors curtain-free.

Throughout the yard, bonsai and rare orchids in Hawaiian pots, my favorites, provide focal points. I move these potted plants around frequently to try out new ideas and combinations. When we have parties, I tend to arrange them on tables indoors rather than buying armloads of cut flowers. They infuse shades of green into the neutrals of the interior, and bringing the outdoors inside in this way appeals to me from a sustainability perspective.

As a home, this place has developed its personality over time. Tending the garden involves a great deal of detail work and all the time I can muster. I love to get out here and move the various elements around. It interests me to explore the possibilities, to change the feel of things. When a space is as contained as this, it is possible to experiment for fun. And it is fairly easy to do that without getting overwhelmed.

BEGONIA 'RED FRED'

Gardens are for living, not just looking. **ABOVE**: Reclaimed pavers from Guatemala feel wonderful underfoot. **OPPOSITE**: Dividing a compact yard into distinct areas can make the overall space feel larger. Hedges and seventeenth-century stone posts do the job here. **FOLLOWING PAGES**: My garden is my laboratory for experimenting with an eclectic mix of unique plant varieties.

RIGHT: For a seamless transition between indoors and outdoors, the tonal value of the wood floors blends effortlessly with the pavers. A Madagascar dragon tree helps bring the outside inside. Simon Toparovsky's bronze Icarus sculpture creates a focal point for the outdoor dining area. **FOLLOWING PAGES:** Plants can be both living architecture and beautiful details that draw the eye.

ABOVE: My dining table often doubles as a buffet. **OPPOSITE**: The succulents live in rare antique Hawaiian orchid pots. I have changed the design of the tabletop several times over the years, but the table base has always been this teak trunk. The lily pond's sheet bronze coping echoes the materiality of my sculpture of Icarus.

Ficus hedges delineate the garden's green "rooms," creating intimate enclosures. In the living area, a reclaimed seventeenth-century stone well contains the fire pit. Atop the brick half-wall, a marble sink contains succulents. In the corner, the crucible used to pour the molten bronze that became Icarus serves as another planter. For year-round use, indoor/outdoor fabric covers the banquette cushion and pillows.

ABOVE, LEFT: My studio opens directly onto our garden bar and kitchen. ABOVE, RIGHT: I arranged this work and entertaining space just like an indoor kitchen. OPPOSITE, LEFT: From the bar, the wood-burning oven offers the same visual appeal as a fireplace. OPPOSITE, RIGHT: The kitchen flows organically into the outdoor dining area.

THE HILLSIDE GARDEN

For house lovers, Los Angeles offers many different opportunities. Always, the final choice is driven by the answer to one very basic question: Would you rather maximize the square footage of the house or of the garden? With this property, a quaint English Tudor-style home on a double lot in the Hollywood Hills, Jean-Louis Deniot and William Holloway have chosen the garden. The two have multiple houses. This is not their biggest. Or their grandest. But it has become one of their favorites because of the way they can live in the jewel box of the house and in the gardens that now give it extended life.

When Jean-Louis and William purchased the property—two lots combined—the gardens called out for a total reinvention. The existing hardscape had crumbled over the years. The hillside—nothing but decomposing granite—was sloughing all the time and falling down the slope. We had to reestablish the hardscape, put in stairways to the house, and carve out pathways that traversed the two lots and wove them together. The only option for accomplishing all that was to create a stepped series of level (or somewhat level) areas on the slope. The process involved introducing garden walls of broken concrete, planted with creeping fig for extra stability and strength, to help hold up the hillside. Then we began installing trees and shrubs in such a way as to keep the water and the soil on the property.

Before we began, this property was all steep slope with very small patios. Jean-Louis and William asked for spaces where people could sit—with room for setting down drinks—as well as others where people could hold plates of food and move around the garden. I wanted them to be able to enjoy multiple areas outside, so we created a series of leveled terraces throughout the property that offer spectacular views of Los Angeles from different vantage points on the hillside. We also installed an outdoor fireplace for lounging and a strolling garden that winds its way directly up and around the house and through the property's upper reaches with additional spots for gathering. This walking tour around the back of the property incorporates a wooden bridge that connects the garden directly to the master bedroom, which allows the owners to enter the yard directly from the second story.

For sustainability, we planted these gardens with California-compatible native materials and irrigated with soaker hoses to keep water consumption down and runoff to a minimum. For seasonal color, we introduced Liquidambar, or sweet gum trees, which turn a gorgeous golden yellow and go deciduous in the fall. When we were just beginning to select the tree varieties, I suggested ginkgoes to Jean-Louis. He replied that the ginkgo was his favorite tree. The oldest known species of tree in existence, it has come to symbolize strength, hope, peace, and enduring friendship because of its resilience and antiquity. We have planted groves of them around the property. They go breathtakingly golden in the fall.

These two tend to entertain with cocktail parties and casual dinners, so we included a productive landscape with allées of Bearss lime trees, lavender, and rosemary. As a result, the garden gives off wonderful scents, especially when people brush up against the plants. Extensive low-voltage lighting placed carefully and practically throughout the landscape makes the gardens safe and functional at night, another nod to the fact that the pair entertain quite a bit.

This garden is as much about function as it is about beauty and sustainability. It has intimate areas for two and comfortable areas for ten. It opens up. It closes down. It changes scale. We designed it to encourage discovery from the street all the way up to the top of the slope, about forty feet above it. Jean-Louis and William say that when family and friends visit and experience all of the garden's different environments, their response tends to be "We can't believe all of this is here on this one property."

Ginkgo biloba

ABOVE: The antique falcon finials chosen by Jean-Louis help frame the entry into the side garden.
OPPOSITE: Boxwood and privet hedges frame the outdoor areas. A casual gravel approach has a country-house feel. **FOLLOWING PAGES:** We shored up the steep slope with a series of broken concrete garden walls, now overgrown with creeping fig, and leveled areas for the garden spaces. Plantings are California natives and compatibles; an espaliered fig climbs the chimney wall.

Simplicity is enormously powerful. I love using basic, essential geometric shapes like squares and rectangles to frame the different areas within a garden. This not only helps to ground each space without distracting from the views, but also plays an important role in establishing an easy, organic sense of flow.

Tight layers of hedges help indicate connections and define access to and from this garden's various individual areas. The lily pond is a perfect square, which so pleases the eye. The fountain contains an antique water spout reclaimed from a demolished Hancock Park residence.

ABOVE: The second-floor master bedroom opens directly to the side yards and a pathway that climbs the hillside.
OPPOSITE: Good space planning for the exterior follows the same rules used for the interior, so I prefer not to mirror the functions of adjacent spaces. Here, the interior dining room flows into the exterior living area.

OPPOSITE: Layers of green at the base of a house help to ground it. ABOVE: A furnished bridge connects the master suite to the gardens. FOLLOWING PAGES, LEFT: A concrete and gravel stairway ascends from the outdoor dining area to the upper viewing gardens; RIGHT: This lounge is a great spot for casual gatherings before or after a meal.

Outdoor entertaining spaces should be integrated so that even people in different areas can see one another and feel that they are sharing the same experience.

SANTA MONICA TRADITIONAL

Some homeowners love to do the unexpected with their gardens. Alexandra Vorbeck is located squarely in that camp, as I discovered while working on this Santa Monica property, our first project together. Alexandra's rather traditional house sits on a conventionally beautiful street in a typically lovely neighborhood—one where the style of plantings in the front yard is mandated. Hedges that completely block the view of the house from the sidewalk are not permitted. Trees and shrubs up to forty-two inches high are allowed. These restrictions inspired us to think differently about how to establish a sense of privacy within a unified vision for the entire landscape—front, side, and back.

Every design has to find its own starting point. This property seemed to call for very purposeful and specific materials, so every decision followed from the hardscape. As soon as we found a reclaimed brick wall from China—all in shades of gray—we knew we had our great beginning. Cut in half and laid in a herringbone pattern, the Chinese bricks form a series of separate pads, like carpets. The bricks led us to a color palette of coral, gray, and white, which upped the complexity of the decision-making process, since all the elements needed to blend well.

To provide layers of screening while still complying with the neighborhood rules, we surrounded the front of the property with a low, painted brick wall and built up the yard a bit so it is all on the same level. A forty-two-inch privet hedge along the wall's inner perimeter and a tier of coral bark Japanese maple trees surrounding the property make the house feel enclosed. In the fall, the maples' leaves turn a gorgeous golden yellow-orange; in the chill of winter, the maples' bark transitions to an intense shade of coral. With the hardscape muted, color truly comes from the landscape. The palette changes seasonally against the dark green backdrop of the privet and the boxwood globes that form a low counterpoint in the front yard.

At the heart of the front garden is a ten-foot-by-ten-foot reflecting pool that centers on the family room and also lines up with the trellis in the backyard. When all the doors and windows are open, the landscape feels as if it is coming through the house. Water lilies infuse the pond with touches of purple in the summer. In the winter, water hawthorn spreads its white buds across the surface. A seventeenth-century stone vessel in the center of the pond creates a little waterfall with a very gentle sound. With dark purple leaves and tiny white flowers, Little John azaleas introduce slight variations into the coral, gray, and white theme.

The Chinese brickwork transitions into the backyard, which unfolds into four comfort zones shaped by privet hedging—a living structure that works as entry, enclosure, and exit. All these areas relate directly to the architecture of the house: The kitchen, dining, and family rooms each unfold into their own separate gardens. A central corridor connects these outdoor areas. At the core is a fire element, the centerpiece of the backyard. Along one perimeter, a lounge area under a steel trellis with lights beckons people outdoors from the family room. From there, the view across the fire garden centers on a wall-mounted water feature we created from a seventeenth-century feed trough. The fourth garden surrounds the pool at the rear of the property. (As the pool had not been touched in years, we replastered the interior and repoured the concrete coping.)

The plant palette extends through the entire property, with the addition of oak leaf hydrangeas in the back. These play into the various whites, so the color story throughout is consistent.

STEPHANOTIS FLORIBUNDA

The story of every house starts at the street. Plants and hardscape can capture the homeowner's personality and help establish a calm space within the urban environment. The front garden is valuable real estate. Why not make the most of it?

OPPOSITE: This fourteen-foot-square water garden is not just a focal point seen from inside the house; it also helps to slow down visitors so they take in the front yard. FOLLOWING PAGES: The sound of water gently rolling over a reclaimed antique stone vessel is very soothing. The plantings change seasonally, with purple tropical water lilies in the summer giving way to white water hawthorn in the winter.

To create some drama in the backyard, I came up with a plant palette that features a combination of oak leaf hydrangea with lavender and agave. The contrasting forms, textures, and colors draw the eye. All are California native or compatible species.

ABOVE, LEFT: I love paring down plant materials and hardscape to the essentials. Boxwood globes add a low layer of green. ABOVE, RIGHT: The custom outdoor coffee tables keep to the palette of beiges and grays. OPPOSITE, LEFT: The repetition of materials feels luxurious but simple. OPPOSITE, RIGHT: The hardscape front and back incorporates carpets of reclaimed Chinese brick set in a herringbone pattern. FOLLOWING PAGES: An environment of boxwood, agave, Japanese maples, and privet screens the pool.

RIGHT: A grid of coral maple trees frames this lounge area. The steel trellis conceals lighting, creates shade, and offers a sense of enclosure overhead. **FOLLOWING PAGES:** Details are consistent throughout. **PAGES 74-75**: The central fire pit anchors the entire back garden and works like a visual magnet to draw people into the exterior.

MODERN MOROCCAN

Design concepts can come in a flash when the owners and the architecture speak clearly. Andrea and Carlos Alberini said from the beginning they wanted a family house to welcome their five grown children, relatives, and friends. They wanted larger outdoor spaces to comfortably seat fourteen. The style of the house—modern with Spanish and Moroccan influences and completely open, with each room offering its own garden opportunity—was just as articulate. Imagining the place as an old olive orchard with a house added later felt right immediately. After I learned that the Alberinis' hometown in Argentina happens to be named Olivos, this idea seemed to make even more sense.

Deciding how the exterior spaces should unfold was the challenge. Erin Martin, their interior designer, and I discussed her use of materials—encaustic cement floor tiles, rich fabrics featuring dark tones with white, and Moroccan elements—as well as the furniture layout, the feel she was creating, and the property's formatting. I developed my palette to complement hers. Most important was the hardscape. Given that we were starting with dirt, the various elements of hardscape had to tie the entire property together. This meant using it to establish the symmetry that the Alberinis love—something the exterior lacked. Erin was using black terra-cotta in parts of the house and for the thresholds. I cut that terra-cotta into thin sections and installed it in a herringbone pattern to define the different garden environments. We outlined her materials and mine in the same black terra-cotta, which made the transitions seamless. Planting a grid of one-hundred-year-old olive trees over the entire property helped to establish a living geometry and the symmetry they desired.

Because it was located on a busy Beverly Hills street, the property needed an enclosed, modern parking court. I wanted it to have a touch of history, too. When I heard about a cobbled road that had been unearthed beneath an asphalt parking lot in downtown Los Angeles, I knew the cobblestones would be perfect for the front and central courtyards. (From a sustainability point of view, it was exciting to find and reclaim something that old from Los Angeles.) Encircled by an olive grove and flanked with symmetrical, graveled parking areas, this entry sets the tone for all that follows.

A second wall to separate the parking court from the entry environment also made sense. This created space in the front for a hello-and-goodbye garden, a planted area where first greetings and final farewells can take place out of doors. Years ago, I had come across some seven-foot-tall columns salvaged from Burrwood, the estate built for Walter Jennings in Cold Spring Harbor, New York, where Frederick Law Olmsted had designed the landscape in 1915 and 1916. Set on a plinth surrounded by boxwood hedging, they perfectly support three arching canopies to create a covered walkway leading to a three-part entry garden centered on a Moroccan-inspired marble water feature. Right outside the house, five-foot-high hedged-off areas seamlessly extend the interiors into the landscape.

The backyard unfolds just as symmetrically. The gallery, dining room, living room, and an office all open directly onto a cobbled central courtyard anchored by a thirteenth-century well converted into a fire element. Here, we introduced the property's one element of hot color and seasonal change, a grid of forest pansy redbud trees that explode with fuchsia blossoms each spring. Once the petals have fallen, dark burgundy leaves unfurl, then transition to green in the summer, and blaze golden in the fall before they drop, waiting for the cycle to begin again.

A cooking area with a large pizza oven also includes an Argentinian grill and a barbecue. This space also incorporates dining for fourteen under a steel trellis enclosed by edible figs and a bar for four. In the heart of the yard, a swimming pool with Moroccan tile provides a cooling counterpoint. We slipped in a glass-walled spa to keep the views open and added an outdoor fireplace on the pool's other side to balance the pizza oven. Symmetry reigns.

BLACK MISSION FIG

PRECEDING PAGES: Framed by a colonnade and paved with custom black terra-cotta tiles, the entry garden makes the path to the Alberinis' front door clear. ABOVE: Stephanotis wraps the colonnade's 1920s-era Frederick Law Olmsted columns, which I found years ago at Elizabeth Street Gallery. OPPOSITE: The custom black terra-cotta hardscape blends with the interior entry floor.

PRECEDING PAGES: In the spirit of a Mediterranean garden, the water in the rills that delineate the entry garden appears to flow from a central marble fountain. RIGHT: This casual sitting area in the front garden is adjacent to the living room. FOLLOWING PAGES: All of the interior rooms open onto this central courtyard, which we paved in cobbles from a turn-of-the-twentieth-century street unearthed during a construction project in downtown Los Angeles. When in full spring bloom, the forest pansy redbuds add the property's one note of hot color. PAGES 88-89: Axial views and symmetry help to give this residence a feeling of expansive comfort.

RIGHT: Off the family room and kitchen, the exterior dining area, bar, and pizza oven offer an opportunity for outdoor entertaining at its fullest. The pizza oven establishes another strong focal point for the backyard. To reinforce the indoor/outdoor connection, we covered its flanking walls in the same Moroccan tile used in the indoor kitchen. Carefully placed one-hundred-year-old olive trees help to create a sense of symmetry. FOLLOWING PAGES: Kumquat trees and French pots from the 1920s add splashes of Mediterranean color to the outdoor fireplace.

THE TIN HOUSE

The opportunity to develop deep roots with the owners of a property, and with the property itself, is a privilege. This is why The Tin House is so special for me. Sue and Alex Glasscock, known for spotting real estate diamonds in the rough and polishing them into sparklers, happened across a five-acre expanse of Malibu hillside not quite twenty years ago. The property once belonged to the artist Ron Davis, who built an exaggerated shed designed by Frank Gehry on it in the early 1970s. In Davis's day, he and fellow artists James Turrell, Robert Irwin, John McCracken, Mary Corse, Larry Bell, and other members of the Light and Space Movement gathered here to explore how geometric shapes and the use of light affected the environment and perception of the view.

The property's role in the history of California Minimalism intrigued the Glasscocks. Although everything about the place was in terrible disrepair, they were able to envision it as a modern ranch. They began to transform it with Michael Lee, their longtime interior designer and friend.

I joined the team as they were putting the house back together. In order to become a home, though, it needed to sit in the landscape in a more residential way. This meant carving out environments in the landscape for entertaining. The Glasscocks also wanted raised-bed gardens for herbs and vegetables, outbuildings for chickens and goats, and a pasture and riding ring for horses.

The property seemed to want to be a refuge, and to do that, it needed to reflect a certain sensibility right from the start. On the street, we set the scene with board-form concrete walls (a classic construction technique that imprints concrete with wood grain) and scaffolding gates to preview the materials of the houses. Gravel replaced the asphalt in a drive that led up the hillside through a new landscape of native grasses dotted with olive trees. Creating a parking court above the house allowed us to establish a casual, comfortable, methodical descent to the front door. This series of steps and landings wraps through the landscape, around a magnificent, existing, California pepper tree, and terminates in a front garden and courtyard of reclaimed cobble. Paving the backyard with the same cobble connects the two areas.

The existing house was almost see-through, with the master bedroom visible from too many angles. A strategically placed board-form concrete wall added definition and privacy, as well as spaces for master and entry gardens. Extending the wall out the house's rear face and down the hillside provided privacy screening from the other direction. Behind the house, the same methodical descent of steps and landings offers an easy, comfortable transition down the slope to the (new) pool area and the property's lower reaches. Here we put the vegetable gardens, space for the chickens and goats, and a horse pasture. (We carved out an acre for a riding ring at the property's top.)

When the Glasscocks purchased their hacienda (see page 198), Patrick and Jill Dempsey took on stewardship of the Tin House. Over the next several years, we reformatted the gardens for their young family. The Glasscocks didn't have a stitch of lawn. The Dempseys, with three young children, needed one as a play area. So the vegetable gardens moved up to the former riding ring, where we added an expansive potting area and a shed, among other things. This freed up the space below for a family fun zone conceived like a good interior. With designer Teak Nichols, we put in an outdoor kitchen with a wood-burning pizza oven and lots of counter space so everyone can share in the cooking. Behind it, we constructed a *tansu*, a pantry-like building for the refrigerator, condiments, and tableware. Installing a steel trellis with a custom willow top nearby gave them dining space for fourteen. A lounge area with a built-in banquette around a fire pit and a great lawn for family games provided a draw to the property's lowermost point.

MORO BLOOD ORANGE

All the materials of the entryway are intentionally casual and approachable, chosen to transport one immediately away from the city. Weathered wooden gates and a gravel drive bounded by wild grasses and other native plantings create an approach to the house that feels like an old rural road. This really sets the stage for what's to come.

When you're trying to blend a garden with existing plantings and an existing house, sometimes you go for contrasting materials. And sometimes you choose a palette that is seamless. The house, the terrain, and the owners' lifestyle always tell you how best to capture the spirit of the place—and the spirit of the owners, too.

OPPOSITE: From the parking courtyard, a walking path winds its way around an existing California pepper tree down to the front of the house. FOLLOWING PAGES, LEFT: Frank Gehry's original corrugated tin cladding gives the house character. With a new pivoting front door and cobble entry courtyard, the house feels casual and inviting; RIGHT: The interior materials palette informed the choice of exterior hardscape.

Look for the ridiculous in everything
and you will find it.

—Jules Renard, 1890

The back of the house is a mirror image of the front. When we began the project, the backyard was just a dirt hillside. We cut into the slope at various points to create carefully retained terraces for the pool area, various areas for other activities, and gardens. The custom broken concrete steps with gravel pads carry the hardscape components from front to back.

ABOVE: Pride of Madeira pulls the blue of the pool water into the landscape. OPPOSITE: Lined with rosemary, flax, westringia, and other California compatibles and natives, custom, broken-concrete steps and walls connect the pool area to the lower terraces. FOLLOWING PAGES: In the second transformation of the landscape, the area at the base of the slope became an outdoor entertaining paradise.

OPPOSITE: Ample built-in seating welcomes family and friends. To reinforce the repetition of materials, I reclaimed scaffolding from around the pool and entry gate. **ABOVE**: A floating stone tabletop is perfect for a drink. With red margin agave, pittosporum, rosemary, and olive trees, this plant palette thrives in the heat. **FOLLOWING PAGES**: Animals are a major part of the lifestyle.

To tie the wood-burning oven
back to the architecture of the
house, we roofed it in
corrugated metal. The warm
hues of the custom stucco
blend naturally with the del
rio gravel and limestone
countertops. The absence of
color is calming and provides
a wonderful background
for the plants to show off their
many shades of green.

FLOWERING DOGWOOD

THE BOULDER GARDEN

The history of a house and its neighborhood can be a rich source of inspiration for a garden, especially when a homeowner wants her landscape to depart from the neighborhood norm, yet still be appropriate to its context. Both conditions apply to Alexandra Vorbeck's boulder garden, which occupies the front yard of her English manor house in Piedmont, a small enclave in the Oakland hills across the bay from San Francisco. Frederick Law Olmsted designed portions of this Northern California community, including Mountain View Cemetery. Established in 1863, it is the resting place of many San Francisco notables, including the architect Julia Morgan. As a city, Piedmont really began to come into its own after the earthquake of 1906, when many San Franciscans fled to its more stable ground.

Piedmont's past remains present in its grand, older homes, most of which are set amid manicured lawns framed by perennials and annuals. My aesthetic is different. Rather than regularly swapping out annuals, my preference is to plant a garden once and let nature take her course, as we have done here.

This house sits on a prominent corner and protrudes high up from the street level, so the landscape needed to ground it somehow and also create more privacy without shutting it off completely from the street view. The neighborhood happens to be built on a large rock outcropping, so it made sense at least to consider the idea of using rocks in a way that felt as if they were excavated from the site. At American Soil & Stone, a prominent stone yard in the Oakland area, we had our eureka moment. The parking lot was filled with boulders the size of minivans, covered with moss and lichen, originally from nearby Napa Valley. After looking all of them over—and climbing some of them, too—we picked out our favorites. These now create a loose, seemingly random seating arrangement under two existing cork oak trees. (Furniture seems so awkward in a front yard.)

The boulders and cork oaks set the stage for an environment that is intended as more of a park than a typical residential landscape; we covered it entirely in local peat and gravel. Piedmont's cooler temperatures and higher elevation allow for the fun of experimenting with a plant palette featuring species other than the Mediterranean, drought-resistant ones that we regularly use in Southern California and love so much. Forest pansy redbuds, red twig dogwoods, and Japanese maples offer the beauty of seasonal color transitions, with particularly magnificent shifts in fall and spring. Instead of skipping grass altogether, we planted no-mow fescue and let it grow wild. Like the boulders, the plants are indigenous, so they fit the larger design concept.

The route to the front door is as unexpected as every other aspect of the garden. There is a definite spot where it makes sense to enter. Various pathways, some marked with pavers sliced from the same family of Napa Valley boulders, connect to the side yards. This encourages visitors to meander through the yard rather than simply heading straight to the entry to the house.

The finished garden is the farthest idea from the traditional front lawn and paved pathway that Piedmont expects. As alternative as it is, however, it has more than proven itself to be appropriate. It is not uncommon to find the neighborhood children playing in the front yard because it has such a hide-and-seek feel to it. When families walk by, the children will often run in, explore the garden quickly, and run out. It is a friendly, welcoming design that creates privacy for the house without saying "keep out." The neighborhood has embraced it.

RIGHT: After wandering among the boulders and trees, the various pathways finally arrive at the front door, which is well-screened from the street. Marking the entry is a random rock that we turned into a water feature—an understated fountain if there ever was one.
FOLLOWING PAGES: Boulders create a usable front-yard seating area without furniture.

ABOVE: Moss-covered rocks from nearby Napa Valley dot the pathways. **OPPOSITE**: Dogwoods and redbuds add traces of seasonal color. **FOLLOWING PAGES**: Specimen Japanese maples form a focal point. **PAGES 124-125**: Though surprising on first view, this front garden's composition, colors, and textures refer directly to the context of the house and its surroundings.

OPPOSITE: We selected and placed each of the Napa Valley boulders that create the garden's distinctive character. ABOVE: Expanses of lichen add another layer of color into the mix. FOLLOWING PAGES: No-mow fescue, boxwood globes, and an irregular stone pathway offer an unexpected take on the typical front garden.

OJAI RETREAT

Some people want their homes to stand out in the landscape. Others, like the homeowner of this retreat, aspire to just the opposite. In response, the design for this property makes use of the idea of "borrowed landscape," which is how exterior designers describe shaping vistas from inside and out to blur the boundaries of where the property begins and ends.

When the homeowner contacted me, construction of this dream retreat—a main house, two guesthouses, a gym, an art studio, and a garage—was already underway on four acres in Ojai, northwest of Los Angeles and directly below Chief Peak, the area's highest summit. At our very first meeting, I began by asking my usual questions: What color is the interior plaster? What materials are the floors? And in what hues? The homeowner, who was not yet working with an interior designer, had no answers. Together we began developing a palette for the interior finishes, pulling all the beige and gray tones from the rocks that dotted the property. To establish a consistent hardscape and give the entire property a very casual feel, we decided on stone and wood floors that matched the gravel. I brought samples of all the materials to the site so we could make sure the transitions between inside and outside would be absolutely seamless.

Based on Ojai's longtime casual vibe and the homeowner's desire to create a place that felt organic to its setting, the aesthetic practically suggested itself. But plant choices were a challenge. In summer, temperatures in this area regularly climb over 100 degrees Fahrenheit, which is to say that the climate is perfect for citrus and avocados, but stresses all sorts of other vegetation. We would need to be judicious in our selections.

The entry to the property lies at the end of a cul-de-sac, behind a plain wooden gate framed by pilasters of local stone and marked by a giant sculpture of a peace sign in bright orange. To give the arrival a processional feel, we threaded a gravel driveway past the outbuildings and up to the main residence. It runs through a series of citrus groves—Kishu tangerine, Eureka lemons, Meyer lemons, limes, Cara Cara oranges, oro blanco grapefruit. (The homeowner, intending to develop jams, was very specific about the citrus varieties.) Grading the surroundings helped to hide the buildings as much as possible behind the stacked boulders that mark the property lines. (All of the stone on the property came from our excavations on site or from a nearby quarry.) Encircling those boundaries with a series of native trees rather than formal hedges or a fence made the entire property feel completely organic to the spot, as if it had always been there.

We wanted to make the main house its own oasis at the property's core. Surrounding it with boulders and plantings and encircling it with gravel pathways instead of formal steppingstones gave it true privacy, but also a certain casualness. We planted the gravel walkways with durable California natives and compatibles: olive and dwarf olive trees, agave, California bay, coppertone loquat, and others, a palette that can thrive in extreme heat and that I first developed for the Tin House.

From a garage that we secreted behind a stone wall, three stairs descend to a graveled front courtyard planted with a grove of olive trees. A reflecting pool helps to ground this area and add a suggestion of coolness. We mirrored this arrangement in the back courtyard, visible straight through the entry and the front door. (The twin water features make a larger statement about how things flow between the inside and the exterior.) All of the iron doors open to the exterior. The only lawn on the entire four acres is a very thin strip of grass around the swimming pool.

The result is a property with a feeling of boundlessness. Because we carefully considered each element visible from every window, the views roll out, and roll out, and roll out to the mountains without stopping.

CLIMBING POLKA ROSE

A landscape with plants that are free to create their own forms can reinforce the rural nature of a property, even when the house is on the more formal side. Natural gravel pathways add to the sense of rusticity and give the experience of walking the property a unique feel.

PRECEDING PAGES, LEFT: Her master bath overlooks a private garden. **PRECEDING PAGES, RIGHT:** His does also, focusing on this water feature. **RIGHT:** This garden encloses the two master baths. All the stone is either excavated from the site or local to Ojai. The wall hides the driveway. **FOLLOWING PAGES:** To keep water consumption low despite the summer heat, we planted the five-acre property with groves of avocados, olives, and California compatibles. The emerald ring around the pool is the only grass on the property.

FRENCH MODERN

I believe that every house starts at the street, not at the front door. From that perspective, the front yard presents an opportunity to set a distinct tone for the property. That is why a manicured lawn may often be the least interesting option from an aesthetic point of view. Grass rarely warrants a second look, much less all the energy, fertilizer, and water that go into maintaining it to perfection. This French-inspired garden is more than just an alternative to the expected patch of green. As a grid of stone, gravel, wood, metal, boxwood, and evergreen pear trees, it obviously alleviates many sustainability concerns. More importantly, it responds to the spirit of the French Normandy-style house with classic modern interiors behind it. Owners Donna and Martin Wolff have filled that house with a stunning collection of modern art that includes works by David Hockney, Ed Ruscha, Roy Lichtenstein, and Sam Francis.

I based the design of the garden on a strict grid of five-foot increments: five-foot-wide stone and gravel pathways, ten-foot-square boxwood hedges, and evergreen pear trees set fifteen feet apart. The regularity keeps people's eyes up and on what's ahead and around them, rather than at their feet. In concept and plan, the result is meant to be as tight and organized as an actuarial table.

Like every French garden, this one focuses on the house. Boxwood hedges nearest the façade introduce the first, low ranks of defining lines. Pathways crisscross the yard from side to side and curb to doorstep in a neat, graphic symmetry, grounding the garden's living elements in a perfect frame. At night, soft lighting magically brings the entire composition to life. Stone pavers quarried in Southern California layer in a shade of gray that complements the exterior of the house. (The stone, called Bouquet Canyon, makes reference to the grand Los Angeles homes of the 1920s, where it was often used.) A perfectly straight custom wooden bench, chiseled like a sculpture, provides not only seating amid the symmetry, but a compelling vantage point from which to contemplate the garden's ordered world. Viewed from the master bedroom that overlooks it, the composition takes on yet another dimension.

Needless to say, when a garden is as mathematical as this one, the installation has to be right on or the effect is lost. As we were putting all the elements in place, my crew and I were fanatical about lining up each edge, plant, and surface. We string-lined. We measured. We checked, rechecked, and checked again.

Mother Nature's palette is not unlimited, and I am not one for a visual riot full of color and texture. Keeping things simple here helps to create a stop-you-in-your-tracks composition that serves as a kind of introduction to the owners' personal world, and to the modern point of view on the other side of the front door.

While working on this garden, for the first time I really began to understand the idea of creating a living architecture in the front yard that relates to both the inside of the house and the people who live in it. This couple has been here for more than thirty years—and they're never moving. This park-like garden, so French and so modern, has become another art piece in their collection. And it still makes them happy.

PYRUS KAWAKAMII

ABOVE: My front gardens never follow the usual formula of lawn and paved pathways. To introduce the owners' modern art collection, this one features five main elements (stone pavers, gravel, and three plant species) placed on a strict grid of five-foot squares. FOLLOWING PAGES: Layers of landscape create privacy; low privet hedges block cars from the interior view without entirely screening the house from passersby.

ABOVE, LEFT: The limited plant palette defines the design. ABOVE, RIGHT: Geometry creates clarity. OPPOSITE, LEFT: A cast concrete planter serves as a water feature. OPPOSITE, RIGHT: Evergreen pear trees add verticality to the garden architecture; their spring blooms contrast with the layers of green. FOLLOWING PAGES: Light has a profound effect, especially in a tightly edited garden.

SPANISH COLONIAL REVIVAL

Sometimes the better part of valor for a designer is to transform a property in such a way that it looks as if it had never been touched. That is my story with this historic estate in Beverly Hills, owned by John and Alison Hawkins. The house, which sits high on a knoll, dates to 1929. Its architect was George Washington Smith, who is known for the gracious Spanish Colonial Revival-style estates he designed in and around Santa Barbara. The house retains all the hallmarks of his exceptional eye and grace, as well as some original details, including ornamental ironwork and a processional driveway entered from the property's left side.

When the Hawkinses purchased the property, they felt very strongly about shepherding it safely into the future. They wanted to improve it without obliterating its past. For me, this meant respecting the history of the house, its materials, and its feel. With each decision, that meant asking myself: If George Washington Smith were alive today, how would he approach it?

Apart from an absolutely spectacular cedar of Lebanon tree, probably John and Alison's favorite thing in the world, the existing landscaping was not particularly inspired. The front lawn unfurled down to the street, which left the house very visible. For privacy and security, the owners wanted to add gates. But putting a gate on the left and running a fence across the lawn, the obvious solution, lacked sensitivity. We finally found a pair of seventeenth-century pilasters to frame the entry to the drive. Paired with a custom iron gate, they feel as though they've been there forever.

To screen the house from the street, I took a Russell Page-inspired approach. Bringing the landscape out toward the street and pushing the street-side perimeter back up toward the house with two retaining walls created more level space in the front of the house for a garden. The retaining walls disappear behind heavy plantings, as does the protective ironwork they hide. A ten-foot-by-ten-foot seventeenth-century stone water feature centered on the front door helps to suggest the idea of a welcoming courtyard. When the front door opens, the axial view ends on another seventeenth-century water element that draws people through the house and out to the back.

The pool was added to the backyard in the 1970s and set nine or ten inches too high; everyone tended to trip over the awkward steps leading from the house to the poolside area. I wanted to make the pool the hero of this environment. We kept the original shape but lowered it and dropped in a spa, glassed-in on one side, to add a modern touch. To give it a feel of history, we rimmed it in five-inch-thick, custom marble coping.

On the left side of the house beyond the living room was a very dark, walled garden. We recentered it on a large reclaimed well converted into a fire element that captures the eye through the French doors. With Arras seating, a coffee table, and a beautiful French lighting fixture overhead, it has become a gentlemen's smoking garden. John's office is right next to it; when his friends visit, they often step into it to play cards and smoke cigars.

A century ago, prominent architects such as George Washington Smith and the homeowners who commissioned them boated pieces back from Europe while their houses were underway. The antiques and specimen trees found at every turn help create the illusion that this landscape dates to the 1920s. To break that vision of the past just a bit, I created a modern bronze sculpture that sits just beyond the front gate. It is one thing that speaks of now—a surprise, but still in context.

PURPLE WATER LILY

PRECEDING PAGES: The front lawn of this historic estate used to unfurl down to the street. For screening, we introduced allées of olive trees and layers of hedges. ABOVE: A custom bronze sculpture introduces a modern flourish into the traditional garden. OPPOSITE: Seventeenth-century pilasters topped by eighteenth-century stone urns add patina and definition to the front entry garden.

With historic properties it is important to respect the past. Blending existing materials with new ones as seamlessly as possible is my way of honoring the legacy of the original architect. What matters most to me is that when my work is complete, the place feels as though I was never there.

ABOVE: From the entry hall, the view to the front garden centers on the water lily–filled fountain at its heart.
OPPOSITE: The vista from the same spot looking toward the back garden encompasses the pool and the seating area with water feature beyond. The symmetry of these dueling water features enhances the interior/exterior connection of this historic house.

Gardens should reveal themselves slowly. That's why creating spots for intimate moments and unexpected places to gather throughout the garden is so important. With seating, lighting, and a source of warmth, a secret garden can become another environment for living and entertaining.

The gentlemen's smoking garden just off John's home office is a great place for him and a few friends to gather when they want to smoke cigars. The seating is vintage Arras from France. One old stone well houses the fire; another, floating above privet hedges, adds a sculptural note. The nineteenth-century French lantern, on a dimmer, further enhances the ambiance.

RIGHT: Adding a period flourish, a custom built-in banquette at one end of the pool incorporates a plaque reclaimed from the Laughlin Park estate of Charlie Chaplin. The chairs are vintage Arras from France. We made the coffee tables by repurposing a pair of stone blocks. FOLLOWING PAGES: Five-inch-thick solid marble coping helps to give the remodeled pool a feeling of old-school architectural glamour. A grid of one-hundred-year-old olive trees creates much needed shady spots in the open landscape.

ABOVE, LEFT: Hand-carved antique limestone blocks house an antique spout. ABOVE, RIGHT: This water element is on axis with the front garden's water lily pond. OPPOSITE, LEFT: The sound of trickling water helps to create an atmosphere of calm. OPPOSITE, RIGHT: The pool coping was antiqued by hand. FOLLOWING PAGES: Antique stone elements and modern bronze ones blend seamlessly with the period architecture.

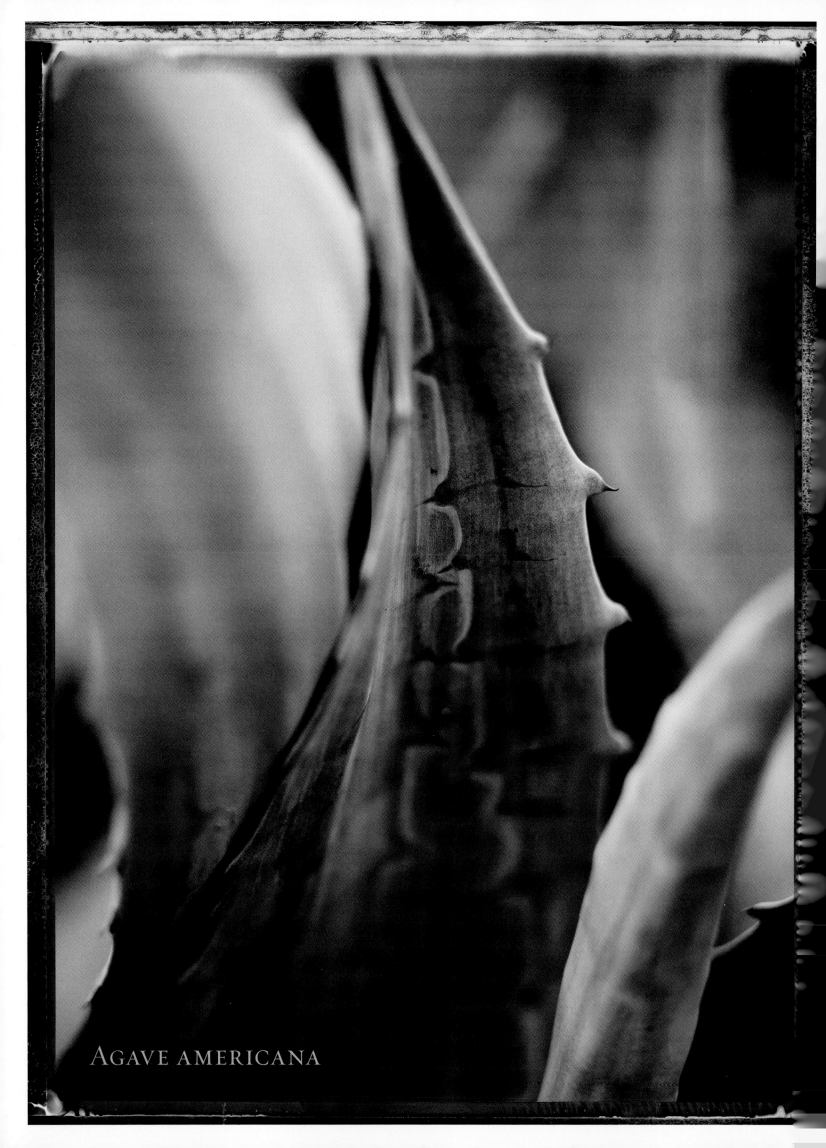

AGAVE AMERICANA

MEDITERRANEAN COMPOUND

Not long before I started my own practice, Lani Berrington, my mentor, and I completed the gardens for this gorgeous, Wallace Neff-designed, Spanish Revival-style house in the flats of Beverly Hills. Neff had created it in 1926 for the concrete baron Lawrence McNeil, whose factory provided all the concrete for the Hoover Dam. Bruce Stuart, who has an eye for historic residential Los Angeles architecture, purchased the house from the woman who owned it after McNeil. He intended to renovate the house in the spirit of Neff's original, while bringing it up to date for his own lifestyle. He was adamant about doing the same with the exterior spaces.

When Lani and I met Bruce, we quickly learned he was truly passionate about gardens and that he would much rather put in a living landscape than a tennis court. He was also trying to come to terms with the fact that the property was simply not large enough to fit everything he envisioned—a guesthouse, pool, greenhouse, and productive gardens. I mentioned that the next-door neighbor's house was for sale and suggested that if he purchased it, we could create a compound of just under one acre that would serve his needs much better. Within three days, he had closed the deal.

For the guesthouse, we worked with architect Steve Giannetti. The idea was to recreate a smaller two-bedroom version of the Wallace Neff main house so that it would look as if it had been there from the first. We sited the new structure at the far end of the compounded lot and designed a sunken lily pool centered in relation to the main house to draw an organic connection between the two structures. Lowering the level of that garden by three steps completely changed its feel and the atmosphere of the

entire outdoor environment. Enclosing the area with a series of traditional boxwood and mature orange trees helped to suggest that there might have been an orchard on the property at one time.

Because the interiors were saturated in very rich shades, we decided to unfold that color story out of doors as well. Establishing bold stands of Brandy roses introduced accents of intense orange into the green landscape. Bruce lost his father before this property was completed, so as a memorial we collected all the rosebushes from his father's house and replanted them here in their own special garden.

In keeping with the original period of the house, expanses of strategically placed lawns helped to paint the exterior with broad, manicured swaths of green interspersed within the hardscape of local Santa Maria stone. The construction of a sizable greenhouse gave the owner the perfect place to indulge his passion for succulents, which we also incorporated into the landscape. A Moroccan-inspired water element in the greenhouse floor brought more Mediterranean flavor into the overall design. We also put in a pool influenced by Spanish precedents—in keeping with the Spanish Revival style of Neff's original design—and a vegetable garden with heirloom tomato vines. And there are nearly a dozen fountains, including a water feature off the entry of the guesthouse that percolates down through the gravel and recirculates. To furnish the various spaces, we used classic outdoor furniture that had belonged to Bruce's father.

With a landscape of succulents, olive trees, citrus, boxwood, lily ponds, and accents of Hermès orange, this garden was definitely a bit of a nod back to old California—and just as definitely a nod to now.

PRECEDING PAGES: With a sunken lily pond and allées of citrus and boxwood, this garden seamlessly connects the two formerly separate lots. The pool coping is made of cast concrete edge pieces typically used for garden pathways. **ABOVE AND OPPOSITE**: Agaves, Carolina cherry, and olive trees give the guesthouse entry courtyard a Mediterranean feel.

ABOVE, LEFT: Local Santa Maria stone grounds the pool and patio area. ABOVE, RIGHT: A new spa was part of the pool remodel. OPPOSITE, LEFT: Garden ornaments sit on the broken concrete stairway. OPPOSITE, RIGHT: The new back garden features a park-like expanse of rolling lawn and incorporates an old retaining wall at the original property line.

An ample stairway now acts as the connective tissue between the two properties. It replaces a concrete-block wall that marked the boundary line.

MIDCENTURY MODERN

Some properties are "It Girls," the stuff of design legend. The Brody house, which dates to 1949, fits this bill. The dream team of architect A. Quincy Jones, interior designer Billy Haines, and landscape architect Garrett Eckbo created the Holmby Hills estate for the philanthropists Sidney and Frances Lasker Brody, who filled it with their world-renowned art collection, including a large tiled Henri Matisse mural in the courtyard. As originally designed, the house merged interior and exterior seamlessly, with wings that extended into the hillside landscape and expanses of windows that opened to well-framed views. When Ellen DeGeneres and Portia de Rossi purchased the property, the house was essentially intact. The interiors still had some original Billy Haines furniture. A number of Garrett Eckbo's landscape features and specimen trees had survived. With interior designer Jane Hallworth, Ellen and Portia, notable art collectors like the Brodys, began redoing the classic, glamorous, midcentury property in a sensitive, stylistically appropriate way. I was brought in to rework the gardens. Given the history, this was a great privilege and a tremendous responsibility.

To honor the estate's modernist origins and its ongoing role as a home for great art, we emphasized simplicity and boldness with repetition of plant materials and striking containers for potted trees. To recapture its original spirit of old Hollywood, we introduced a combination of boxwood globes with carefully chosen additional species. Boxwood globes help delineate the front entry, which opens to an entry court still paved in its original black and white terrazzo. Instead of replacing it, we decided just to polish it to a soft glow. A black olive tree set in a seventeenth-century stone container planted with a sea of sansevieria adds life and character to the space. As a reference to the Brodys' famous Matisse, we decided to spotlight one of Ellen and Portia's sculptures, a carved stone horse. Because the sculpture seemed to ask for an unusual form of display, we placed it in what was once a planter and set the planter atop a plinth encased in sheet bronze.

In the interior courtyard, we introduced a carefully selected dining table by Blackman Cruz. A large crucible that we converted into a planter became home to a very gnarly succulent. We reupholstered some of the existing Billy Haines furniture in simple black and reused it here as well.

Behind the living room, which echoed the midcentury aesthetic, was a glass atrium—never easy to landscape. This kind of space always requires very selective choices. Here, we had to consider that it served as a backdrop to the side of the living room anchored by a commanding painting by Sean Scully and three François-Xavier Lalanne sheep. A moss garden introduced intense color and velvety texture. An enormous staghorn fern, hung from a very heavy chain, added spraying fronds of green that fanned out behind the various artworks.

In the backyard, along with original trees and an expansive lawn, a beautiful water element had survived, though it was not quite intact. We were able to resurrect it, and planted Wheeler's dwarf pittosporum around its base to give it a living frame. Strategically positioned containers planted with succulents give the yard some subtle definition and color variation. One wall—a very sculptural focal point framed by an interior window—called for a particularly strong composition. We found another staghorn fern, set on a piece of wood that hangs on the wall; we planted liriope grasses below.

The guesthouse had a marbled spa. For the adjacent garden, as a nod to mindfulness, we veered in a slightly Japanese direction. Here a bonsai pine tree planted in an old concrete container suggests age and calmness. Surrounded by baby's tears and liriope grass, the area took on a modern Zen feel, not quite midcentury, but not far from it, either.

DIOSCOREA ELEPHANTIPES

PRECEDING PAGES: To live up to the property's stellar design pedigree, the landscape needed to be highly refined. **RIGHT**: Boxwood globes in gravel beds create an organized approach. The uniformity and simplicity of the approach help give importance to the front doors, which still wear their original, Billy Haines–designed hardware.

ABOVE, LEFT: The Billy Haines-designed hardware has such great charm. ABOVE, RIGHT: At the entry, a black olive tree in a stone vessel stands out amid mass plantings of sansevieria. OPPOSITE, LEFT: The water feature is one of the few surviving elements of Garrett Eckbo's original hardscape. OPPOSITE, RIGHT: This giant staghorn fern gives a blank wall a focal point, just as an art piece would.

Simple and spare, the spa plantings are reminiscent of those found in Japanese gardens. A massive antique bonsai helps to anchor the modern, minimal space and give it a sense of age and history.

THE HACIENDA

When old Hollywood plays into the story of a property, the facts can be juicier than fiction. This two-hundred-acre ranch set high in the hills above Malibu, with Boney Mountain as a backdrop, is a perfect example. William Boyd, aka Hopalong Cassidy, built the hacienda as a getaway spot sometime in the early 1910s. (He came by horse; the building materials, by mule.) By the time Sue and Alex Glasscock purchased the place, it had gone entirely to seed. Just as they remodeled the interior of the hacienda to suit their family lifestyle and entertaining needs, we created an organic exterior architecture of hardscapes and plantings that shape environments for (and connective pathways between) living, dining, and lounging that radiate seamlessly beyond the walls of the house. Almost before we did anything else, we relocated the house's front door so that the cinematic procession of arrival would have a proper moment of reveal into and through a garden. Over time, we have also reconfigured and replastered the pool, built a pool house that doubles as a guesthouse, constructed a wall of stacked stone that, along with hardy native species, lines the driveway, and installed gates to mark the passage into the entry. A private herb garden off the kitchen, plus an orchard and acres of organic gardens add the required grace notes.

With so much surrounding land, the only way to work was in phases. Once we developed a master plan that outlined the priorities, the transformations happened in increments. Areas closest to the house came first, with a focus on carefully planned material transitions—such as those between terra-cotta tiles custom-made in Mexico to match the originals, stone excavated from the site for walls, and shades of wall plaster to match—that tie the interior and exterior together seamlessly. Area by area we placed and tended a palette of native Californian and California-compatible plants and trees into garden environments for

living that unfold through the larger landscape as naturally as possible. The back patio pushed the living room into the open. Just beyond the kitchen door, we planted herb gardens in raised beds built of stone from the site, added a potting area, and created a space shaded by a trellis with cup of gold vines that dresses up nicely for large lunches. Atop a stepped walkway lined with dwarf olives we identified a space perfect for a formal dining environment beneath a trellis ablaze with different colors of bougainvillea. A graded slope on the dining area's farther side descended logically to the pool—plastered a custom shade of taupe pulled from the surrounding hills—a small spa, and the pool house/guesthouse.

Dwarf olives—the go-to for our understory because they require so little water, resist insects, and can take lots of sun—frame many of the outdoor living spaces and line the pathways between them. Cypress, which grows rapidly and is just as tough, adds a green vertical element against the olive's silvery gray-green. Along the stone walls that line the driveway, we planted an allée of young oak trees that should grow into their full might in twenty or thirty years; a low, native ceanothus introduces a hint of blue into the mix of greens and earth tones.

Because the property lives off two wells, thinking sustainably about irrigation and focusing on hardy species were givens from the outset. We also built a small water reclamation plant for sewage treatment, and some of that water is used in place of well water to irrigate.

Digging to plant led to numerous surprises, as the entire spread rests upon the solid rock of the hillside. The overall scale of the spread called for sizable plant material—and lots of it. To date, we have tamed or touched eighty acres in a timeless, ranch-style design meant to endure; the back forty will most likely remain wild, just as nature made them.

DOUBLE WHITE ANGEL'S TRUMPET

I love to create the intrigue of entry.
When there is a cinematic procession
of arrival, there should also be a proper
moment of reveal into and through
a garden. What's most important, though,
is that there be absolutely no ambiguity
about the location of the front door.

PRECEDING PAGES: From its site high up in the Malibu hills, the hacienda has a spectacular
view of the Boney Ridge Traverse. OPPOSITE: Flanking pilasters, a custom gate, and dramatic,
carefully placed agave specimens make the point of entry to the inner courtyard clear.
Terra-cotta hardscape in a herringbone pattern gives the approach a classic, timeless feel.

A front garden should capture the spirit of the house and the personality of the owners. There is nothing more welcoming than an open front door, especially when it offers a view straight through the house to the back garden and the vista beyond.

When we started the project, the front entry was just dirt. Now it is warm, embracing, and relaxed—in keeping with the character of the hacienda and its new owners. A pair of olive trees reach warmly to all those who arrive at the front door. Vintage terra-cotta planters and old stone pieces blend with the architecture.

OPPOSITE: The reclaimed well is a perfect water bowl for Clara and Pip. Old olive trees form a magical canopy of welcome. **ABOVE**: This Agave salmiana's mother plant lives at the Wallace Neff house; her pups have found homes here and on several other properties. **FOLLOWING PAGES**: With a trellis that replicates the original architecture, the rear garden blends seamlessly with the house.

ABOVE: The ample kitchen has a timeless, modern feeling. OPPOSITE: Just beyond the door are raised beds for vegetables and herbs, an area for a casual intimate meal, and a potting area with a sink.

RIGHT: The backdrop for the potting area is built of stone from the site. The sink is a repurposed old stone planter.
FOLLOWING PAGES: The raised beds for the kitchen gardens and the network of low walls are all built with stone materials found on the property. We incorporated a seating area into the wall because I never want to miss an opportunity to encourage relaxation and taking in the view.

ABOVE: These side gates open to the gardens and pathway that lead to the swimming area. OPPOSITE: A casual dining pavilion off the herb garden centers on the view. FOLLOWING PAGES: From goats to chickens to dogs and more, the animal life helps to define the character and function of this two-hundred-acre property.

OPPOSITE: The archway on the upper terrace forms part of the connection that joins the pool area with the main house. Oak, cypress, and dwarf olives create a lush but sustainable environment around the swimming pool. ABOVE: Nestled right next to the pool is a private spa.

RIGHT: The ample garden spaces offer many different options for outdoor entertaining. The entry courtyard doubles as a dining area when weather permits.
FOLLOWING PAGEs: The pool house also serves as a guesthouse. What guest could ask for more?

RINCON POINT

Alexandra Vorbeck loves transforming properties as much as—maybe even more than—I do. She is always looking for another challenge. When she found this beach house property north of Los Angeles, she could not resist. The entire property was in very sad shape. The county had recently condemned the house—relocated from Carpinteria, California in the 1960s—which had been built mostly on sand without any footings or foundations and added on to haphazardly over the years. The existing gardens included only one semi-functional outdoor space, a pagoda. A sunken pond occupied the sweet spot for commanding the view, a long vista to one of California's great surf breaks. But the location—just a short walk from the beachfront, and next to a tidal lagoon—was perfection. Alexandra imagined turning it into her own private Idaho of a retreat to share with family and friends: the ultimate California-casual getaway, suited to a dress code of T-shirts, shorts, and flip-flops.

To be here is to want to interact with the water, air, and views, day and night, from all points on the property. To make that possible we used materials that bring the feeling of the shore right up to the threshold of the house and visually extend the experience of the living spaces to the beach and water beyond.

In order to give direction to the large gestures and small details of our redesign, I developed a story of a tsunami landing on the house. When it passed, it left the house engulfed in an almost accidental landscape of randomly scattered boulders (in a practical touch, these serve as impromptu seating), drifts of sand, and an assemblage of boardwalks that tie the house and gardens together. Working with architect CJ Paone, we opened up the interiors of the house with axial views, focal points, and moments that reflect the ocean, and we planked the walls and ceilings (picking up the boardwalk theme) to create easy, breezy, light-filled rooms visibly in sync with the surroundings. Beyond the walls, we casually integrated layers of function with environments conducive to lounging, casual dining, conversation, and just hanging out—a fire pit; an easy area for four to six to share a meal, play cards, or shuck oysters; a larger lounge area for bigger groups; plus, of course, the numerous boulders that offer incidental places to sit or put down a drink.

Since we wanted a random effect, it did not make sense to plot every single plant and every single position obsessively. We knew the plant palette had to consist of drought-tolerant salt-lovers native to California. We knew we would create an arbor of fig trees off her master and find a worthy specimen—which turned out to be a strawberry guava—to commemorate the birth of her first granddaughter. I sketched in the boardwalks with a can of spray paint. We figured out the basic structure for the landscape. With four large trees—including a spectacular, mature Monterey cypress—still standing proud, we began to shape our vision with the understory, arranging Metrosideros to grow into a hand-clipped screen around the property's perimeter. Interspersed are fifteen additional Monterey cypress trees, planted in homage to their elder and intended to add, eventually, similarly impressive tall shafts of green.

While the house and garden were still under construction, Alex held a "naming" party to select a moniker for the house. The unanimous favorite? The Sandbox. We have now guided The Sandbox through the process of becoming for more than five years. As it continues to mature over the next thirty or forty, my hope is that it will be demonstrated that we have planned well for its future—and that, with care, it will only continue to grow more and more into its best self.

EUPHORBIA LAMBII

A garden by the beach offers all sorts of design opportunities. But why not keep it simple? There is something so special about stepping barefoot off a platform into sand. Maybe it's the way you suddenly immerse yourself into the landscape. Or maybe it's just the way the sand feels against bare feet.

OPPOSITE: This house offered the perfect opportunity for a boardwalk garden, a first for me.
FOLLOWING PAGES: Because this is a family retreat, it felt right to keep things casual and easy.
PAGE 232: A console holds beach finds. PAGE 233: A seating area between the main house and the guesthouse is one of several spots for impromptu gatherings.

ABOVE: Once the entry to the house, this spot is now the most private area on the property. It's also the best vantage point for viewing the gardens and the surfers who ride one of the area's best surf breaks.
OPPOSITE: The console is made from stone stairs repurposed from the property. A zinc planter turned upside down serves as a coffee table and footrest.

ACKNOWLEDGMENTS

I'd like to fondly thank:

My dad, Richard Shrader, who leads by example and nurtured a solid platform for me to become the man I am today. My mom, Maureen Shrader, who always knew I was special. My husband, Mark Hemphill. You're the one I was always looking for. Kind, generous, spiritual, loving, unpretentious, compassionate, forgiving, trusting, devoted, and the best baker in the world.

Julie Milligan, you're the sister I always wanted. I love and adore you. Paul King and Gary Murphy of Tudor Stone & Brickwork for more than twenty years of amazing hardscape work; your team has brought my work to such a beautiful level.

Lani Berrington, who gave me my start and introduced me to the world I was always meant to live in. I'm so thankful our paths crossed. The Vazquez family, for your twenty-five years of hard work and dedication. I could not have created these gardens without you. Lisa Collins, thank you for helping to design my website and more. To DiDi, for showing me how to really fall in love and live without fear. Sue Glasscock of the Ranch at Live Oak. You're the first client I fell in love with. Your style, openness, curiosity, and heart-stopping charm are ever so captivating. Alexandra Vorbeck, a spirit who's projected me forward in so many ways. I adore what we have created together. You own a special part of my heart. Michael Lee, the uber talent who introduced me to Sue and Alex Glasscock. Our work together has been amazingly uplifting. Barbara Wiseley of Formations and Dennis & Leen for opening my eyes more than any other. Her belief in me was life changing. Jean-Louis Deniot for writing such a beautiful foreword.

Donna and Martin Wolff for taking a risk with an unknown young designer. Your garden really helped me gain confidence early on. My dearest Terry Haljun, master gardener, you are much closer to my kind than anyone. We see each other's souls and I'm so grateful to have created a garden with you. You are a dream. Solange Williams, you're the most beautiful woman, inside and out. Chris and Lisa Bonbright of Café Gratitude and Gracias Madre, you're two amazing humans I've loved growing with. Carlos and Andrea Alberini, I'm honored to know you and so proud of the garden we created together. Greg and Kathi Hansen, truly two of the loveliest people one could ever have as clients. Alison and John Hawkins for trusting me with your spectacular home.

Lisa Romerein, the photographer's photographer, you were the first to photograph my work in 2002, putting me on the map. Your amazing eye blinds me with joy. Mark Adams, such a talent. You found and captured the image of my Roxy, to whom this book is dedicated, on the day of her rescue. I'm ever grateful. You're one talented photographer and kind human being. Richard Bloom for your wonderful photography abilities.

Hicham Murr of La Maison Francaise Antiques. Your garden space is my home away from home. My work wouldn't be the same without you and your knowledge and devotion to the quest for antiquities. Jesse Castaneda, a talented and soulful architect, your ability to research beyond all others warms me. Your lack of ego is priceless. Peter Messinger for being my water feature guru. Adam Blackman and David Cruz of Blackman Cruz, the birthplace of the impeccably couture home and garden necessities that ground my own home. You two rock. Who's any cooler than Ray Azoulay of Obsolete, may I ask? Tom Henry of Orchids de Oro for your wicked passion and unique eye for beauty. Stephen Block of Inner Gardens for bringing Los Angeles the best garden adornments. Ryan Hroziencik of The Tropics, a wonderland of unbelievable specimen plant material that will take your breath away. Charles Thomas at Berylwood Tree Farm, the specimen nursery with a history worth knowing. Durling Nursery, family owned citrus and fruit growers in Fallbrook since 1926 and world-class citrus growers; when your refrigerated truck arrives on site, everything changes for me. Jack Mayesh at Kobata Growers. Thirty years providing me with excellent material. Rudy Ziesenhenne, the Santa Barbara genius of begonias. Yours is a legacy I'd love every landscape lover to know. The Santa Barbara Orchid Estate, which offers an experience beyond imagination where orchids become living art. Rafael Shamouelian of My Garden for your tenacious work ethic and ability to find me beautiful specimens consistently. Allan Reiver of Elizabeth Street Gallery in New York. Shawn Benavi and James Brunning with Stoneland for your amazing attention to detail and being one of my best go-to sources for stone. Exquisite Surfaces for bringing reclaimed stone and wood to the Los Angeles market in such a chic and respectful way. Thanks to a man way ahead of his time, Mike Riley of Lewis Unique Wrought Iron, for thirty years of wrought iron and steel trellis work. You are the only one who could master the twist and hand-knotted detail. Erin Martin, designer and major force.

Jill Cohen, the gatekeeper, for bringing my work to Rizzoli's attention. Doug Turshen and David Huang for designing such a beautiful book. Judith Nasatir for your most beautiful words. Stephanie Flood for keeping my books and not judging on the frequent occasions when we finish accounting day with a large glass of Chardonnay.

I'd like to also thank the publications, including the editors and writers, who have graciously published my gardens over the years: Susan Heeger and Barbara Thornburg from the former *LA Times Magazine*; *Martha Stewart Living*; the fantastic Andrea Stanford of *C Magazine*; Thad Orr with *Garden Design*; Mayer Rus with *Architectural Digest*; *Luxe Interiors + Design*; and Clinton Smith with *Veranda*.

And a very special thank you to my publisher, Charles Miers, and my editor, Kathleen Jayes. I'm honored to be part of the Rizzoli family.

First published in the United States of America in 2019
by Rizzoli International Publications, Inc.
300 Park Avenue South
New York, NY 10010
www.rizzoliusa.com

Photo Credits:
All photography by Lisa Romerein with the exception of the
following pages:

Richard Bloom: page 16

Mark Adams:
pages 4, 59-75, 96-97, 104, 110-111, 147-153, 189-197

Design by Doug Turshen with David Huang

2019 2020 2021 2022 / 10 9 8 7 6 5 4 3 2 1

Distributed in the U.S. trade by Random House, New York

Printed in China

ISBN-13: 978-0-8478-6359-4

Library of Congress Catalog Control Number: 2018959594